THE BRITANNICA COMMON CORE LIBRARY

WHAT IS A

DISCARD

PLAY?

JENNIFER CULP

Britannica®
Educational Publishing

IN ASSOCIATION WITH

ROSEN
EDUCATIONAL SERVICES

Published in 2015 by Britannica Educational Publishing (a trademark of Encyclopædia Britannica, Inc.) in association with The Rosen Publishing Group, Inc.
29 East 21st Street, New York, NY 10010

Distributed exclusively by Rosen Publishing.
To see additional Britannica Educational Publishing titles, go to rosenpublishing.com.

First Edition

Britannica Educational Publishing
J. E. Luebering: Director, Core Reference Group
Mary Rose McCudden: Editor, Britannica Student Encyclopedia

Rosen Publishing
Hope Lourie Killcoyne: Executive Editor
Nelson Sá: Art Director
Nicole Russo: Designer
Cindy Reiman: Photography Manager

Library of Congress Cataloging-in-Publication Data

Culp, Jennifer, author.
What is a Play?/Jennifer Culp.
    pages cm. — (The Britannica Common Core Library)
Includes bibliographical references and index.
ISBN 978-1-62275-668-1 (library bound) — ISBN 978-1-62275-669-8 (pbk.) — ISBN 978-1-62275-670-4 (6-pack)
1. Theater — Juvenile literature. 2. Drama — Juvenile literature. I. Title.
PN2037.C85 2015
792 — dc23
                                                                    2014023034

Manufactured in the United States of America

Photo Credits: Cover (background) © iStockphoto.com/marcoventuriniautieri; cover (hands and tablet) © iStockphoto.com/Anatoliy Babiy; cover (tablet screen), p. 1 © iStockphoto.com/ferrantraite; p. 4 Jero Morales/EPA/Landov; p. 5 Kike Calvo/Visual & Written/The Image Works; p. 6 Michael Sofronski/The Image Works; p. 7 Jordan Pix/Getty Images; p. 8 © Elliott Franks/ArenaPal/The Image Works; p. 9 © Nobby Clark/ArenaPAL/The Image Works; p. 10 © Warner Bros./courtesy Everett Collection; p. 12 (left) Hope Lourie Killcoyne; p. 12 (right) © Louise Batalla Duran/Alamy; p. 14 De Agostini/Getty Images; p. 15 James Keyser/The Life Images Collection/Getty Images; p. 16 Simon Hayter/Toronto Star/Getty Images; p. 18 Fedor Selivanov/Shutterstock.com; p. 19 The Asahi Shimbun/Getty Images; p. 20 Heritage Images/Hulton Archive/Getty Images; p. 21 Freer Gallery of Art, Smithsonian Institution, USA/Robert O. Muller Collection/Bridgeman Images; p. 22 © AP Images; p. 24 George Karger/Pix Inc./The Life Images Collection/Getty Images; p. 26 Musei Capitolini, Rome, Italy/Alinari/Bridgeman Images; p. 27 Alinari/Getty Images; p. 28 Avava/Shutterstock.com.

What Is a Play?

A play is a story that is acted out before an audience. Plays are often performed in **theaters**. "Drama" is another word for "play." Unlike most other forms of literature, plays are meant to be shared with many people at once.

Different styles of plays exist throughout the world. In many cultures in Asia, dance, gestures, and music in a play can be as important as the words that

Theaters are places where people go to see plays and other performances.

Costumes and makeup are often important elements of a play.

are spoken. Asian plays are often based on familiar stories and tend to have a formal style.

Western dramas usually tell a story through dialogue, or the conversations that the characters have with one another. Western plays follow two main styles: tragedy and comedy. Tragedies are serious stories of struggle that often end sadly. Comedies are amusing stories that often have happy endings. Today many Western plays mix elements of tragedy and comedy.

Some plays tell a story with movement and dance instead of words.

5

How and Why Are Plays Performed?

Plays can be about any topic. They are written to be performed for an audience. A play's performance provides people with an entertaining and shared experience. The experience moves people to think and feel more deeply about life.

Often, many tasks must be done before a play can be performed. Some of these tasks include the creation of scenery, costumes, and lighting. Actors must memorize words, actions, and any

A crew member works behind the scenes to keep a play running smoothly.

music. Large productions have a director. The director studies the written play closely and directs actors, designers, and **stagehands** on how and when to complete their tasks.

All the people in a play must do their part at the right time. The audience, too, plays a role by listening, watching, and not interrupting the shared experience.

Stagehands are people who prepare the scenery and lights of a stage for a performance.

A play can cause its audience to feel many different emotions.

Elements of a Play

The writer of a play is called a playwright. The major elements of a play include the characters and the plot. The characters often come into **conflict** with each other over something. The plot is what happens during the play. It shows how conflicts are settled.

The characters' words and movements tell a play's story. A playwright might write dialogue to match how people of a particular

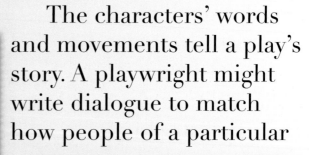

Conflict means a struggle or disagreement.

In stage combat, actors pretend to fight or even kill each other without actually doing any harm.

time and place actually spoke. Or the dialogue may follow a certain style. Examples include when characters' words are written in poetry or when characters are expected to sing or chant words.

Stage directions tell the actors how to move and interact with each other.

The playwright also writes short instructions, called stage directions, in the text. Stage directions tell the actors what to do or describe what a character looks like. They also describe the time and place of the action. The play's designers use these descriptions to create the scenery, costumes, and lighting.

Reader's Theater

Where the Wild Things Are, by Maurice Sendak

Before performing *Where the Wild Things Are* for a kindergarten class, a group of fifth-grade students wrote a **script**.

A **script** is the written text of a play that includes stage directions, character descriptions, and dialogue.

A **rumpus** is a state of noisy and exciting activity.

Where the Wild Things Are *was adapted into a live-action movie in 2009.*

Below is their version of the "wild **rumpus**."

SETTING: a forest at night with a full moon

[Enter **MAX** wearing his wolf suit and king's crown, followed by the WILD THINGS.]

MAX (growling) Let the wild rumpus start!

[**WILD THINGS** immediately let out fierce howls. They continue to snort and growl for the rest of the scene.]

MAN-FACED WILD THING (claws at the full moon as if trying to catch it) Waaabawabawaba gluh! (continues clawing and chanting)

THREE-HORNED WILD THING (joins in on trying to catch the moon) RRRRRRRah! RRRRRRAWWWW!

MAX (ignoring the others, howls a repeated chant of his own) Zaba Wuba Huh-Huh!

The Ugly Duckling, by Hans Christian Andersen

Augusta Stevenson wrote scripts of many well-known stories. Here is the beginning of her first scene for *The Ugly Duckling*.

The duckling in Andersen's tale goes through many struggles before turning into a beautiful swan.

Well-known folktales are often adapted into plays for the stage.

TIME: one summer morning.
PLACE: the farmyard of the Moor Farm.
CHARACTERS:
MADAM DUCK, FIRST DUCKLING, SECOND DUCKLING, THE UGLY DUCKLING, THIRD DUCKLING, TURKEY, GRAY GANDER, WHITE GOOSE, PLYMOUTH ROCK HEN, RED ROOSTER

[**MADAM DUCK** enters the farmyard with her new **brood** of **DUCKLINGS**. The other **fowls** approach.]
TURKEY (showing displeasure) A new brood of ducks! Look you all—a new brood of ducks!
GRAY GANDER (also displeased) As if there were not enough of us here already!
WHITE GOOSE (likewise displeased) True enough,—I can **scarce** find a corner for my afternoon nap!
RED ROOSTER. It seems to me, Madam Duck, that you should not have brought us a new brood this summer.
MADAM DUCK. What is that you are saying?

brood: young animals or children in a family
fowls: birds
scarce: hardly

13

Let's Compare

Hans Christian Andersen wrote The Ugly Duckling *and many other famous children's stories.*

The scripts for *Where the Wild Things Are* and *The Ugly Duckling* retell famous stories for the stage. Each script has stage directions and follows basic rules that all scripts must follow.

Character names always appear in all capital letters. Whatever a character says follows his or her name in regular type. Whatever a character does appears in parentheses after that character's name.

Stage directions can appear after a character's name or begin their own line. Stage directions must appear in parentheses or brackets. They may appear in **italics** so that they are not confused with words that the characters say. Character names that are mentioned within stage directions must appear in all capital letters.

Italics is a form of type that slants upward to the right like *this*.

Playwrights

James M. Barrie's play *Peter Pan* was first performed in 1904. Barrie revised the play many times. Its final version was published in 1928.

Maurice Sendak wrote and illustrated the children's picture book Where the Wild Things Are. *It was first published in 1963.*

Romeo and Juliet,
by William Shakespeare

William Shakespeare wrote *Romeo and Juliet* in about 1594–96. The play's plot was taken from a poem Shakespeare had read. The story tells of two young people who fall in love. Because their families are long-time enemies, though, the two people are not allowed to be together. The dialogue on the following page takes place during a secret meeting between the young people.

The balcony scene, as this scene is known, is one of the most famous parts of Romeo and Juliet.

JULIET	Romeo!
ROMEO	My dear?
JULIET	At what o'clock to-morrow Shall I send to **thee**?
ROMEO	At the hour of nine.
JULIET	I will not fail: 'tis twenty years till then. I have forgot why I did call thee back.
ROMEO	Let me stand here till **thou** remember it.
JULIET	I shall forget, to have thee still stand there, Remembering how I love **thy** company.
ROMEO	And I'll still stay, to have thee still forget, Forgetting any other home but this.

> **thee:** you
> **thou:** you
> **thy:** your

Kagekiyo, by Zeami

Noh is a type of drama that was developed in Japan in the 1300s. Noh plays present classic Japanese legends using movement, music, and words. A man named Zeami is considered the greatest Noh playwright. On the following page are the first lines in Zeami's *Kagekiyo*.

In Noh performances some of the actors wear special stylized masks.

GIRL and ATTENDANT
Late dewdrops are our lives that only wait
Till the wind blows, the wind of morning blows.

GIRL
I am Hitomaru. I live in the valley of Kamegaye. My father Kagekiyo the Passionate fought for the House of Hei and for this was hated by the Genji. I am told they have **banished** him to Miyazaki in the country of Hyūga, and there in changed estate he passes the months and years. I must not be downcast at the **toil** of the journey; for hardship is the lot of all that travel on unfamiliar roads, and I must bear it for my father's sake.

attendant: servant
banished: sent away
toil: struggle

For hundreds of years, women were not allowed to perform Noh plays. Men performed both male and female roles.

19

Let's Compare

The passages from *Romeo and Juliet* and *Kagekiyo* demonstrate different ways of telling a story onstage.

In the passage from *Romeo and Juliet*, Shakespeare uses dialogue to show how much the two characters love one another. Neither character wants to say good-bye, and they keep forgetting that's what they are doing.

In the passage from *Kagekiyo*, the playwright Zeami uses two traditional approaches. The very first words of the play

Principum amicitias!

William Shakespeare is often praised as the world's greatest playwright. Though he lived 400 years ago, his plays are still studied and enjoyed today.

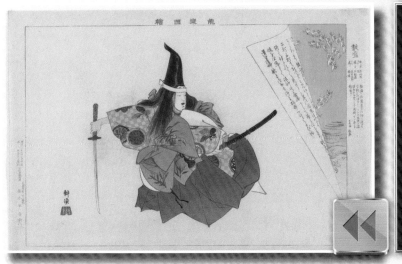

Hitomaru's aside to the audience explains events that have led to the situation at the play's beginning. Her aside will help the audience understand what happens in the play.

are said by two characters at once. The words they speak are formal and poetic: "Late dewdrops are our lives." Their words express an overall feeling. The girl then introduces the story as an **aside**.

Both passages use language that sounds different from the language you may be used to hearing. In both cases, the language gives an idea of the world the characters live in.

An **aside** is a comment spoken by a character in a play that is heard by the audience but not by other characters.

Oedipus the King, by Sophocles

Sophocles' tragedy *Oedipus the King* was first performed in ancient Greece in about 430 BCE. As the story unfolds, Oedipus investigates a murder and discovers something terrible about himself. A chorus (group of actors) describes what happens and

In ancient Greek plays, the chorus provides explanation and dialogue to help the audience understand the play's plot.

JOCASTA   Ah **mayst thou ne'er** discover who thou **art**!

OEDIPUS   Go, fetch me here the **herd**, and leave **yon** woman
                To glory in her pride of ancestry.

JOCASTA   O woe is thee, poor **wretch**! With that last word
                I leave thee, henceforth silent evermore.
                [Exit JOCASTA]

CHORUS   Why, Oedipus, why stung with **passionate** grief
                Hath the queen thus departed? Much I fear
                From this dead calm will burst a storm of **woes**.

comments on it. In the passage above, Queen Jocasta begs Oedipus not to investigate further.

mayst thou ne'er: may you never
art: are
herd: herdsman
yon: that
wretch: unhappy person
passionate: easily angered
hath: has
woes: troubles

Frogs, by Aristophanes

The comedy *Frogs* was first performed in 405 BCE. In it, the god of drama, Dionysus, wants to bring back a dead playwright from the underworld. Charon, the ferryman to the underworld, coaxes Dionysus to row in time to the croaking of frogs.

Actors in ancient Greek plays wore exaggerated makeup and masks.

DIO.	Why, how am I to pull? I'm not an oarsman, seaman, ...I can't!
CHAR.	You can. Just dip your oar in once, You'll hear the loveliest timing songs.
DIO.	What from?
CHAR.	Frog-swans, most wonderful.
DIO.	Then give the word.
CHAR.	Heave ahoy! Heave ahoy!!
FROGS	Brekekekex, ko-ax, ko-ax!
	Brekekekex, ko-ax, ko-ax!
	We children of the fountain and the lake
	Let us wake
	Our full choir-shout, as the flutes are ringing out,
	Our symphony of clear-voiced song.
	. . .
	Brekekekex, ko-ax, ko-ax.
DIO.	O, dear! O, dear! Now I declare I've got a bump upon my rump.
FROGS	Brekekekex, ko-ax, ko-ax.
DIO.	But you, perchance, don't care.
FROGS	Brekekekex, ko-ax, ko-ax.

25

Let's Compare

The passages from *Oedipus the King* and *Frogs* are ancient. They represent two original forms of Western drama: tragedy and comedy.

In the passage by Sophocles, the story is told through dialogue between Oedipus, Jocasta (his wife), and the chorus. In ancient Greek theater, the chorus was a group of actors who described and commented on the main

Aristophanes was a master of comedy. It is believed that he wrote a total of 40 plays. Only 11 of those works have survived. They are still performed today.

action of the play. The chorus's role involved song, dance, and speaking. Here the chorus notices that Jocasta is strangely upset and declares: "From this dead calm will burst a storm of woes."

In the passage by Aristophanes, the frogs take the place of the chorus. Their chirping adds to the overall comic mood of the play. They do not seem helpful or concerned with Dionysus's struggle to row to the underworld.

Playwrights

Geraldine McCaughrean has written all kinds of literature, including many plays for young people to perform.

Sophocles was a master of tragedy. Some of his most outstanding characters were women, such as Antigone and Electra.

Write Your Own Play

1. Think of a story that you want to tell. Will you write a script of a story that you have read? Or will you use your own plot? Summarize the plot in a short paragraph.

2. Define your characters. Make a list of character names. Describe what these characters want, how they relate to one another, what they look like, and how they move and speak.

3. Define your setting. Describe it in details that will help create scenery for the stage.

When you write a script, you imagine the story and how it will be performed. There is no limit to how creative you can be.

4. Imagine the play performed onstage. Write down what you imagine. Describe the actions and dialogue.

5. Follow the rules for writing stage directions and dialogue. Put stage directions in parentheses. Make sure that characters' names are placed before their words and appear in all capital letters.

6. Read through your script with a friend or two. Revise the script as you read to clear up any confusing parts.

7. Revise it some more until it is ready.

8. Gather your performers and stagehands. Practice the play again and again.

9. Invite your audience and perform!

GLOSSARY

actor A person who performs the script of a play for others.

characters A person in a story in a story, novel, or play.

chorus A group of singers and dancers in Greek drama who take part in or comment on the action.

comedy An amusing story that often has a happy ending.

dialogue A conversation between two or more people.

drama A piece of writing that tells a story and is performed on a stage.

literature Writing that is considered to be a work of art.

playwright A person who writes plays.

revise To make changes to something in order to correct or improve.

scene A division of a play that presents continuous action in one place.

setting The place and time in which the story of a play takes place.

stage directions Instructions to actors written into the script of a play.

tragedy A serious story of struggle that often ends sadly.

Books

Bany-Winters, Lisa. *On Stage: Theater Games and Activities for Kids.* Chicago, IL: Chicago Review Press, 2012.

Beechum, CC. *Shakespeare for Kids: Four Plays Adapted to Perform with Kids.* CreateSpace Independent Publishing Platform, 2012.

Hal Leonard Corp. *Broadway Songs 4 Kids.* Montclair, NJ: Hal Leonard, 2011.

Peterson, Lenka, and Dan O'Connor. *Kids Take the Stage: Helping Young People Discover the Creative Outlet of Theater.* New York, NY: Crown Publishing Group, 2010.

Rhodes, Immacula. *Folk & Fairy Tale Plays for Beginning Readers: 14 Easy, Read-Aloud Plays Based on Favorite Tales That Build Early Reading and Fluency Skills.* New York, NY: Scholastic Teaching Resources, 2010.

Websites

Because of the changing nature of Internet links, Rosen Publishing has developed an online list of websites related to the subject of this book. This site is updated regularly. Please use this link to access the list:

http://www.rosenlinks.com/BCCL/Play

INDEX